THE SOVIET UNION

by
Gail B. Stewart

CRESTWOOD HOUSE
New York

Collier Macmillan Canada
Toronto

Maxwell Macmillan International Publishing Group
New York Oxford Singapore Sydney

Library of Congress Cataloging-in-Publication Data
Stewart, Gail. 1949-
  The Soviet Union / Gail B. Stewart. — 1st ed.
    p. cm. — (Places in the news)
    Summary: Examines the Soviet Union's changing political scene, status as a superpower, and relationship with
the United States.
    ISBN 0-89686-537-1
    1. Soviet Union—Politics and government—1985- —Juvenile literature. 2. Soviet Union. I. Title. II. Series:
Stewart, Gail, 1949-   Places in the news.
DK288.S74   1990
947.085'4—dc20   90-38408
                                                                                                        CIP
                                                                                                        AC

Photo Credits
Cover: Peter Arnold, Inc.: Dieter Blum
Magnum Photos, Inc.: (G. Peress) 4; (Dacat) 16, 32; (S. Salgado) 20; (Lessing) 26; (Rene Burri) 29;
    (Costa Manos) 36; (St. Perkins) 39; (Franco Zecchin) 43
AP—Wide World Photos: 10, 13, 23

CRESTWOOD HOUSE

Macmillan Publishing Company   Collier Macmillan Canada, Inc.
866 Third Avenue   1200 Eglinton Avenue East
New York, NY 10022   Suite 200
                                      Don Mills, Ontario M3C 3N1

Produced by Flying Fish Studio Incorporated

Printed in the United States of America

First Edition

10 9 8 7 6 5 4 3 2 1

CONTENTS

On Revolution Day in 1989, Soviet protestors interrupted patriotic celebrations with demonstrations demanding democracy.

THE SOVIET UNION IN THE HEADLINES

On November 7, 1989, a very unusual parade took place in Moscow, the capital of the Soviet Union. In fact, there were two parades going on at the same time. One was made up of marchers carrying government signs, with slogans praising Soviet leaders. LONG LIVE OUR LEADERS! read their signs. THE COMMUNIST PARTY IS THE REAL LEADERSHIP OF THE SOVIET SOCIETY!

The other parade was quite different. Its marchers were critical of the government. Some of their signs called Soviet leader Mikhail Gorbachev a fake. Others read: THE 1917 REVOLUTION WAS A TRAGEDY! and DEMOCRACY IS WHAT WE WANT!

What was going on?

In the Soviet Union, November 7 is a national holiday. It is called "Revolution Day," after the revolution, or overthrow, of the government that took place on that date in 1917. Similar in spirit to America's Fourth of July, Revolution Day is a day of celebration, parades, marching bands, and speeches.

In 1989, however, the holiday was different. It wasn't a time of national unity and pride but a day of confusion, anger, and for some, embarrassment.

Because the Soviet Union is so large, many of its republics were to have their own celebrations. There are 15 republics, or states, that make up the Soviet Union. Each republic has its own legislature, but each is under the control of the central communist government.

On Revolution Day in one republic, Moldavia, several thousand people broke through the lines of police and marchers. They wanted their own demonstration, but it was one to criticize, not celebrate, the central government. The government leaders who had come to watch the festivities left in a hurry when they saw the angry mob. The parade was abandoned.

In some republics, officials had predicted that angry demonstrators would cause trouble, so Revolution Day celebrations were canceled even before they began.

But the largest, most important celebration took place in Moscow. There, in Red Square, hundreds of thousands of people turned out to see the marchers and the dozens of military bands. They also were eager to see the tanks and powerful weapons that the army always displayed on such occasions.

However, in Moscow, as in many of the republics, there was tension. More than ten thousand demonstrators began their own parade, although riot police did not permit the demonstrators to enter Red Square. While the regular parade marchers wore bright red armbands, the demonstrators wore blue ones.

Not long ago, such demonstrators would have been tortured, killed, or sent to a prison in Siberia, the coldest part of the country.

This event made front-page news in many newspapers around the world. People everywhere were astonished that the Soviet Union's leaders were not very angry about the demonstration. In many countries, citizens have the freedom to speak out against what they believe is wrong. The Soviet Union, however, has never been one of these countries.

People were even more surprised when President Mikhail Gorbachev admitted during an interview at the march that the

demonstrators had a reason to be impatient. He acknowledged that his reforms were moving slowly. He also noted that it was important to put an end to complaining. Hard work, not demonstrations, would be the key to progress, said Gorbachev.

Political analysts, people who study the way governments work, know that changes are happening very quickly in the Soviet Union. Nations closely allied to it are also greatly affected. Countries like Poland, Czechoslovakia, and Romania are voicing their strong desire to break away from communism. They say that the communist economic system does not work. And they want freedom and democracy.

Many political analysts think that the Soviet Union is on the brink of some drastic changes. "They are coming to a point of no return," said one specialist in Soviet politics. "It will be the most interesting story of the new decade—to see how the Soviet Union will handle its almost impossible problems without losing the confidence of its people."

What are the "almost impossible problems" that the Soviet Union is facing? Is there reason to believe that the nation is not the superpower it has appeared to be since World War II? And what does the United States think about the changes going on? How will they affect relations between the two countries? Exploring these questions will help explain why the Soviet Union is making such exciting news today.

GORBACHEV'S SOVIET UNION

Mikhail Gorbachev has been the leader of the Soviet Union since 1985. In that time, he has made sweeping changes. He has introduced new ideas and inspired much-needed reforms in industry, agriculture, and the media.

Perestroika and Glasnost

Gorbachev is a loyal Communist. He believes that private ownership of business can be harmful. He supports the communist philosophy that says all property should be shared. But he is also well aware of the problems in his country. He knows that the system of government is very bureaucratic. That is, it suffers from too much time-consuming paperwork and "red tape." He knows, too, that many Soviet citizens are impatient with an economy that does not give them enough food, shelter, or clothing.

After taking office, Gorbachev introduced a new approach to government. He summarizes it with two Russian words, which he hopes will inspire the Soviet people. The first word is *perestroika*. It means "restructuring." Gorbachev wants to reshape the Soviet economy, which has been suffering for many years.

In a few ways, he has already done that. He has allowed some people to start private businesses, such as hospitals. He has encouraged farmers to set aside some of their land for their own

Mikhail Gorbachev has made many important changes in the Soviet Union since taking control in 1985, including allowing some private businesses to operate and opening relations with the West.

10

use. The government still dictates what farmers grow on the state and collective farms. But now farmers can do as they please on the other land.

This idea seems to be working. These "private plots" are small, but they are tended with loving care by the farmers. The government allows the farmers to keep some of what they grow. However, a good portion of it is sold in markets. Some recent statistics show how much more efficient farmers can be with private plots. Although they make up only 2 percent of the farmland, the private plots are yielding more than 30 percent of the fruits and vegetables sold in Russia.

The second word Gorbachev uses is *glasnost.* It means "openness." For many years, the Soviet government has not been open or honest with its people. It often has changed the news that was reported to Soviet citizens. The changes made the Soviet Union look good and its enemies look bad. Often people were misinformed about important events of the day.

But no matter how honest and open he is, Gorbachev has big challenges ahead. By encouraging honesty, he has given the green light to citizens to speak up. They can start their own newspapers and discuss issues freely. They are being permitted to criticize the government. This has never been allowed before, not in the history of the Soviet Union.

Yet this honesty has brought forth frustration, anger, and impatience. Now that Soviet citizens can speak up, they have a great deal to say, and most of it is unfavorable.

"Gorbachev's *glasnost* is a solution, but it's also one of the biggest problems," writes one political expert. "Whether he can survive all that honesty will be the true test of the man."

Criticism from Both Sides

Gorbachev is being criticized by many Soviet citizens for moving too slowly. At the same time, he is being rebuked by others—many of them Communists in the government—for going too fast. They say he is allowing too much change and, thereby, putting communism in danger. "If he does not watch his step," says one government official, "he will be more American than the Americans."

One event that brought such criticism was a recent strike by Soviet coal miners. The miners are paid well, but they were angry for other reasons. Mining is dangerous, they argued, but there are ways to make it safer. In other nations, safety devices are used to decrease the risks miners face. In the Soviet Union, however, the government never bought these safety devices. In the last nine years, ten thousand Soviet miners have died in accidents.

The strikers also complained of shortages. Meat, dairy products, and toilet paper were hard to get. And soap! In one of the grimiest occupations, these miners complained, they were allowed only one bar of soap every two months! Changes had to be made, the miners said, and they had to be made quickly. When the government bureaucracy was slow to respond to their demands, the miners called a strike.

These Soviet miners were like pioneers. Strikes were new. They had never been allowed before in the Soviet Union. But under Gorbachev's policy of *perestroika* and *glasnost*, the miners believed that they could strike and that the government had to give in to their demands.

Under Gorbachev, strikes, like this one by miners demanding better working conditions, are legal. At one time, these strikers would have been jailed for speaking out against the government.

13

In this case, the government did give in. However, Gorbachev's critics worry that strikes will become common now that the government has given in once. What will it do if farmers or electrical workers strike? What will happen to the idea of communism if the workers are allowed to fight for more money? After all, in a communist society like the Soviet Union, the government is the employer!

Relations with the United States

Since World War II, the United States and the Soviet Union have been considered the world's two superpowers. That means they are the strongest, most powerful nations in the world. Both countries have mighty armies and supplies of powerful nuclear weapons. Their decisions affect many people. Because the two nations have almost continually clashed about world events, many people have long feared a dreadful, devastating war.

Both the United States and the Soviet Union understand the enormous power they have. Leaders of both nations insist that they want to live peacefully with each another. However, there are people on both sides who distrust the other. Some Soviets think the United States cannot be trusted; some Americans believe the same about the Soviet Union. Both sides point to events in history that, they say, prove the dishonesty of the other.

One big obstacle dividing these two countries is that they have very different ideas about how people should live. Each country believes that its system is right.

The Soviet Union is a communist society. In it, all property is owned by the state. Communists believe that private ownership of businesses or property is unfair, because some people become rich while some are poor. They believe that communism is fair for all, since all property is owned by all the people. In theory at least, a communist society has no classes—no rich, middle, or poor. Everyone is equal.

The United States, on the other hand, is a capitalist society. That means that property is owned by individuals. In theory, anyone in a capitalist society, by working hard, can make a lot of money.

Much of the change happening today in the Soviet Union has to do with the people's dissatisfaction with communism. Since the whole country is based on that system, it is important to understand how it works and how Soviet leaders came to choose that system in the first place.

THE STORY OF SOVIET COMMUNISM

The Soviet Union is the largest nation on earth. It is, without question, the leader of all communist countries. In fact, it was the first country to make the theory of communism a reality. Until 1917 the communist system had never been tried.

15

Before becoming a communist country, the Soviet Union was a nation of poor farmers ruled by a small group of wealthy landowners.

16

Before it became a communist country, the Soviet Union (or Russia, as it was then called) was ruled by powerful czars, or emperors. There were no lawmaking bodies or courts to advise the czars. They had strict, absolute authority. Those whom the czar disliked were imprisoned or killed.

Russia at that time was a land of two classes, the rich and the poor. The czar and a few wealthy landowners were the upper class. And the vast majority of the population—over 80 percent—were poor farmers, called serfs. Unlike the small farmers, or peasants, in Europe, who were poor but free, these people were slaves to the landowners. They did all the work of growing the crops and caring for the farm animals. In return, the landowners gave them tiny plots on which to grow their own food.

Serfs were considered property, not human beings. A land-owner could beat or kill them if he was dissatisfied with them. They were never paid for their work.

During the time of the czars, Russia was considered the most backward country in Europe. Its agricultural methods were primitive. Its political ideas and culture were far behind those of other nations. During the exciting time of the Renaissance in Europe, for instance, many nations enjoyed a rebirth of literature, art, and music. Ideas about the rights of the individual person emerged. But in Russia, according to historians, it was still the "Dark Ages."

There was a reason for the ignorance of the Russian people: The czars wanted them that way. It was far easier to control people who could not read or write. The serfs did not communicate with the rest of the world. They had no chance to dream of a better way of life. They had no ambitions. They simply tried to stay alive despite the cruel conditions into which they were born.

From Country to City

The serfs were finally freed in 1861—they were no longer the "property" of the landowners. Czar Alexander II freed them. He was eager to reform many of the harsh rules the serfs had had to endure. The czar gave them the chance to buy land from their former masters.

However, this did little to improve their lives. Most of these peasants could not afford to buy the land outright, so they made monthly payments. If a peasant failed to meet one payment, the landowner could take back his land. The peasant and his family were forced then to beg forgiveness from their "master." The master usually forgave them, on the condition that they return to working as serfs for him, just as before.

By the end of the 19th century, Russia had finally developed a few industries. Hundreds of thousands of peasants left the hard life of the farm. Some moved to mining communities; others went to cities, where they worked in factories. The new living conditions, as it turned out, were just as bad as the old ones. In the cities, for instance, poor working families lived in crowded, dirty little rooms, sometimes separated from another family only by a burlap screen. The wages for factory work were low. Many families starved or grew sick from lack of good food.

Because Russia was a land of so much inequality—a country of a few rich and many poor—it is not surprising that there was a great deal of discontent. In 1917 the people rose up against Czar Nicholas II and forced him to abandon his throne. After several months, however, the new government was in trouble. Russia was in the middle of World War I, and there were shortages of just about everything. No one had enough food; no one had material to make clothing. There was no fuel for stoves, and people seemed to have given up hope.

Many small groups of revolutionaries had formed by 1917. Each group wanted to take advantage of the situation and gain control of the government. The group that finally did seize power was led by a man named Vladimir Lenin. He and his followers were called Bolsheviks. They believed that the only hope for Russia was to throw out the old system of government. A new system—one fair to all—must be adopted.

Marxism

Lenin was a believer in the ideas of a German named Karl Marx. Marx thought that capitalism was wrong because it put power in the hands of greedy, selfish people. Under capitalism, said Marx, the people with money controlled everything. Whoever owned the factories, the farms, and the land made the decisions for the nation. The poor people who worked on the farms and in the factories got little in return. The owners alone kept making more and more money and acquiring more and more power.

Marx developed a theory, called communism. According to this theory, if the factories, the land, and the farms were put into the control of the government, no one would be richer than anyone else. Everyone in society would be equal. According to Marx's theory, everyone in the community would share the profits.

Lenin and his followers believed that the idea of communism could work in real life. He and the Bolsheviks (who later renamed themselves the Communists) persuaded the people that their new

system would work. Lenin used the slogan "Peace, Land, Bread." Those words appealed to the tired, frustrated workers. They followed Lenin, and this led to the November 1917 revolution that made Russia a communist nation.

A Difficult Change

Lenin was considered a great leader. He had the ability and energy to lead people from a life of poverty to a life of purpose. The change to communism, however, was not an easy one. It was not accomplished in Lenin's lifetime.

Many drastic measures had to be taken to make Russia a communist country. All land that was held by landowners had to be seized by the government. Factories, businesses—even homes— were taken by the workers, and the former owners were thrown out.

There were problems with this sudden change. For one thing, one cannot simply remove the leaders of a business and expect the business—or government—to function as before. Careful attention must be given to finding new leaders.

Unfortunately, this did not happen after the Russian Revolution. Many businesses were almost ruined by new leaders who had no idea what they were doing. When Lenin died in 1924, it was clear that the change to communism had to be slower and more thoughtful. However, Lenin's successor was not a patient man.

Every year on Revolution Day, the Soviet people hold celeb in praise of Lenin, the man who established communism ir

The Man of Steel

Russia became known as the Soviet Union in 1922, although many people use the two names interchangeably. The man who rose to power in the Soviet Union after Lenin was Joseph Stalin. Stalin was not his real name; he chose it because it means "steel" in Russian. He wanted a name that sounded strong and forceful.

Stalin ruled the Soviet Union with just such a steel grip until his death in 1953. He had a firm idea of how the country should be run. He vowed that he would rapidly turn his backward nation into a world power. He also wanted to spread the system of communism to all industrial nations of the world.

When Stalin came to power, peasants were still using wooden plows. Often women and children pulled them when horses and oxen were scarce. The output of industry was low, and methods were far from modern. To survive as a power in the modern world, Stalin believed that his country had to become a leader in industry. The Soviet Union had a lot of catching up to do.

Stalin devised a series of five-year plans for quickly developing the Soviet Union. These were economic programs with specific goals, each over a five-year period. Although Lenin had seen that communism could not be forced upon the Soviet Union overnight, Stalin was in a hurry. He had no patience for those who moved slowly. What had been started—and slowed down—under Lenin was speeded up under Stalin.

Joseph Stalin was a harsh and unpopular leader who ruled the Soviet Union by imprisoning or killing anyone who did not agree with his ideas.

Angry Peasants

One of the first things Stalin did was to take the farmland away from its owners. He combined many small farms into a few large ones. He thought these would be more efficient to run. However, the farmers who had owned the land were furious. They either had inherited the land or had worked and saved to buy it. Why were they being told they must give it to the government? And to make matters worse, they were told they must sell their harvests at low, fixed prices to the government!

Many of the farmers objected to the new plan. They were angered by the idea of government officials telling them how to run their own farms. When they were told the government was coming to take over their livestock, some of the farmers butchered their animals and sold the meat.

While farm production suffered, industry skyrocketed under Stalin. New factories, mines, and chemical plants sprang up. Big dams were built, and hydroelectric stations were opened. Stalin built up the Soviet Union in a very short time. Using the muscle of a huge work force, he brought the country into the 20th century. But while Stalin accomplished a great deal, he did so, historians say, at the expense of many people.

A Government of Fear

Stalin was neither loved nor admired. He was a hard, cruel leader. He demanded complete loyalty from his people. Those who criticized his ideas, became—in Stalin's mind—enemies. For Stalin's vision to succeed, his enemies had to be removed.

He "removed" them by killing, torturing, or imprisoning them. Anyone who spoke a word against Stalin's ideas was in danger of losing his or her life. He encouraged people to spy on each other. Friends spied on friends; workers spied on workers. Children were even taught to turn in their own parents!

And who were the enemies of Stalin? Historians report that as many as 40 million people were killed or imprisoned by Stalin! These large-scale attacks against Soviet citizens were known as purges. Such mass arrests and murders made the Soviet people fearful and suspicious.

Stalin counted among his "enemies" political opponents, people who believed the government was not being run the way it should be. Those who failed to do their jobs correctly were also considered enemies. For example, one Soviet citizen remembers a family friend who was sentenced to ten years of slave labor. What was his crime? The fruit wagon he was driving was too slow and the fruit rotted during the journey to market!

Distrust and the Cold War

World War II began while Stalin was in power. The Soviet Union joined with the Allies—the United States, Great Britain, and France—to defeat Germany. But after the war, this alliance fell apart.

Hitler's German army had conquered much of Europe. The first order of business after the war was to divide up the conquered lands. The Allies, including the Soviet Union, agreed t

Nikita Khrushchev, who led the Soviet Union after Stalin's death, continued the cold war against the West.

just in this division. They wanted to promote peace and freedom as they redesigned Europe's boundaries.

However, the Soviet Union did not keep the bargain. It remained in many of the Eastern European countries its armies had freed from Germany. The Soviet Union worked hard to establish communist control in these nations. Once communism was adopted, the Soviet Union could, as a world communist leader, be a controlling force. The Soviet Union eventually controlled seven nations of Eastern Europe, including Poland, Romania, Czechoslovakia, Hungary, and East Germany.

In 1945, at the end of the war, the Allies had agreed that the Soviet Union could establish control in the eastern part of the German capital of Berlin. The United States, France, and Great Britain agreed to oversee the western part of Berlin. The city of Berlin lies well within the borders of East Germany. West Berliners needed assurance that they would have freedom of movement between their city and West Germany. However, the Soviets went back on their word and tried, in 1948, to cut off Berlin by blocking all roads leading west. The United States, France, and Great Britain responded to this blockade by flying thousands of tons of supplies into West Berlin. After 11 months, the Soviets lifted the blockade.

Because the Soviet Union had broken its word about working for peace and freedom in Europe—and because of the Berlin action—relations between the United States and the Soviet Union grew tense. Several incidents drew the nations to the brink of war, but each time war was averted. Although the armies of the two nations did not actually fight, their leaders fought a cold war. This means that they were hostile to each other, and angry words were spoken. The United States and the Soviet Union neither trusted nor liked each other.

Changing Attitudes

After Stalin died, Nikita Khrushchev became leader of the government. Historians say that Khrushchev relaxed his grip on the country. The purges stopped. The Soviet Union was allowing its people a little freedom.

The cold war continued under Khrushchev and did not begin to thaw until he was forced out of office. During the administration of Leonid Brezhnev, a policy of somewhat friendlier relations with the United States was begun. This policy was called détente. During détente there was more trade between the two nations. In 1972 the United States and the Soviet Union signed a treaty limiting nuclear weapons. However, many factors, like the Soviet invasion of Afghanistan in 1979, continued to keep the two superpowers at odds.

It was not until the rise of Mikhail Gorbachev in 1985 that tensions began to ease. His thinking seems to be different from those who came before him. Guided by his new *glasnost* policy, he has spoken out against the evils of the past. He has admitted that the Soviet Union made a mistake in Afghanistan and in other nations as well—something a Soviet leader has never done.

Gorbachev has improved his country's relations with the outside world. But the greatest challenge he faces today is coping with the many problems that exist within the Soviet Union itself.

Mikhail Gorbachev has put an end to the cold war and now encourages friendly relations with the West. Here, he and his wife, Raisa, host a visit at the Kremlin with the Ronald Reagans.

PROBLEMS INSIDE THE SOVIET UNION

At the heart of the Soviet Union's trouble is its economy. Workers are not being paid enough for the work they do. The country does not have enough money to pay for a decent health-care system. Consumers complain that even when they have money, there is nothing to buy. The communist system is not working.

The Country That Cannot Feed Itself

One of the most severe problems in the Soviet Union is its agricultural system. During the time of the czars, millions of serfs farmed the land. So much food was grown, in fact, that Russia was able to export food to other nations.

However, under communism, the Soviet Union has not been able to feed itself. Today the Soviet Union imports more grain than any country in the world. Many Soviet people feel that this is shameful. They point out that their country has more land devoted to farming than any other nation.

Historians say that the trouble began in Stalin's time. The dictator was so eager to catch up to the industrial technology of the United States and Western Europe that he ignored his country's farmers. The smartest and most creative Soviets were put to work designing new weapons and new kinds of factories. Funds that should have been used to modernize farms were used for building up the army and industries. These were more important to Stalin than agriculture.

No Private Farms

There are two kinds of farms in the Soviet Union—*kolkhoz* and *sovkhoz*. A collective farm, called a *kolkhoz*, is actually many farms combined. About four hundred families live on such a farm. They pool their machinery, livestock, tools, and supplies. The *kolkhoz* farmers do not own the farm, however. It is owned by the government, and the farmers pay rent.

These Soviet farmers find that their work is almost entirely controlled by the government. The government tells them what to plant, and how much. They must meet certain production guidelines or risk being penalized. After the harvest, the government buys the crops at low, fixed prices.

The other kind of farm is called a state farm, or *sovkhoz*. A *sovkhoz* is larger than a collective farm. One is usually about 50,000 acres. *Sovkhoz* workers do not lease the land, as do *kolkhoz* farmers. The state farms are owned and operated by the government. Those who do the work on state farms are not really farmers. They are hired workers, paid as factory workers are paid. As on collective farms, the government takes the crops and controls the price of their sale.

Farm production in the Soviet Union declined dramatically under the communist system. Today farmers contend with old equipment, outdated methods, and, most importantly, a sense of despair.

32

"Farming in a Prison"

Although the Soviet farms are impressive in size, they are very inefficient. Those who have visited farms in the Soviet Union report that farmers are not interested in their work. Because they have no say in what goes on, they take no pride in the quality of the crops they grow. They get paid to do the tasks the government sets for them. It really makes no difference whether the crops grow or not. What matters is that the workers follow the directions of their superiors.

One agricultural expert from the United States who visited the Soviet Union was astounded by what he saw. Piles of unused food for livestock lay rotting in the fields. Tractors and other expensive farm machines stood idle. Soviet farmers told the visitor the machinery could not be used. It had been purchased from other nations, and the Soviets could not fix the machinery when it broke. Spare parts were not available, so millions of dollars' worth of machinery sat rusting in the rain.

Many people think that because all decisions are made for the farm workers, they do not care whether things get done. Anatoly Strelyani, an agricultural expert in the Soviet Union, believes the system is at fault. "You work for a bureaucrat instead of for yourself," he says. "You cannot show initiative or talent. This makes the farmer indifferent to the land. It's unnatural to farm in a prison."

Many agree with him. One Soviet farmer admitted his heart was not in his work. "I am a very little cog in a very big machine," he said sadly. "I am no different than a worker in an assembly factory. I work outside, that is all. The fruits of my work are not my own."

Sour Milk and Spoiled Fruit

There are other reasons why Soviet farms cannot produce enough food for the country. Much of what is produced is wasted. One problem is delivery. Less than 20 percent of the roads in farm areas are paved. Many roads are no more than muddy ruts through the fields. Workers hauling the produce to market often have long delays.

Because of such delays, milk often turns sour before it reaches the market. Fruit rots. The workers have no choice but to throw the food away, and that means less food for consumers to buy. Experts estimate that almost one-third of the dairy products, fresh fruits, and vegetables are lost because of these delays!

"This Is the Store That Has No Meat"

There is a popular joke in the Soviet Union. Like most Soviet jokes, it is funny because it is true. It tells of a woman who goes into a store in Moscow.

"I'd like to buy a few eggs, please," she says to the man behind the counter.

"I'm sorry," he replies. "You came into the wrong store. Across the street is the store that has no eggs. This is the store that has no meat."

The inefficiency and waste of the farming system have a big effect on all Soviet people. None of the grocery stores ever seem to have enough on their shelves. People stand in line just to buy a few basic supplies, such as butter or meat. One Soviet writer estimates that the average Soviet citizen spends about an hour and a half each day on lines!

Grocery stores operate in a much different way in the Soviet Union than in Western countries. For instance, in an American grocery store you shop first and then pay. In the Soviet Union, you must first stand in line and pay for what you want. Then you have to line up again with your receipt. Each counter in the store—vegetables, meat, dairy—has a separate line.

All the while, store loudspeakers blare. They announce to shoppers whenever the store is close to running out of a certain item. If (as so often happens) the counter runs out of something you've already paid for, you must stand in line again to get your money back!

Because in most families both the husband and wife work, quite often the job of standing in line falls to a grandmother or grandfather. Few people ever leave home without a little shopping bag, called an *avoska*. The bag is well named, for *avoska* means "just in case." If one runs across something good, or just happens to be around when a store is stocking the shelves with a hard-to-get item, the *avoska* will come in very handy!

Often a Soviet citizen will spot a line and get in it without knowing why. The idea is, if there is a line—especially a long one—the item must be valuable. If the shopper doesn't need the item himself, he can surely sell or trade it later to someone who does.

Shortages of food and goods of every kind have made lines like this one a part of everyday life in the Soviet Union.

Not Just Food

Food is not the only item for which Soviets stand in line. There are shortages of many things. Good, comfortable clothing (especially blue jeans), appliances of all kinds, and even sneakers are very hard to come by. This angers many Soviets. They feel frustrated, for even when they earn a good living, there is nothing to spend their money on.

Some stores do have limited supplies of brand name jeans and sneakers from the United States. However, these are available only to high government officials or important members of the Communist party. Some items can be purchased on the illegal "black market," too. Black market goods are expensive—often selling for ten times their original value.

"A Video Uprising"

People in the Soviet Union are getting more and more fed up with the lack of consumer goods. Recently in Yaroslavl, an industrial city north of Moscow, there was a large disturbance over VCRs. Officials called it a "video uprising."

Several stores had the VCRs but were allowed to sell them only to people who had foreign currency. (Some factories in the Soviet Union do business with other nations and are paid in those nations' currencies.)

But consumers heard about the VCRs and objected. Why should these valuable items be sold only to those with foreign money? they asked. Hundreds of people lined up outside the stores. Many began hunger strikes, threatening to starve themselves to death. They hoped to call attention to the unfairness of the situation.

Eventually the stores relented. The first shopper finally walked out of a store, his new VCR raised above his head. "Victory!" he shouted. "The Panasonic is in my hands!"

The Health of Soviet Society

Another problem facing the Soviet Union today concerns the health of its people. New statistics are coming out which show that the Soviet Union is not a healthy place in which to live.

Fresh water is not available to everyone. In fact, more than 30 million Soviet citizens must use water that is not considered safe to drink. Some of this water may contain particles of lead or other metals. Some may contain traces of fertilizers or other chemicals that farmers put into the ground.

Chemicals and metals build up in the bloodstream and can cause serious diseases such as cancer and lead poisoning. Soviet officials know that the water is unhealthy. However, it costs a great deal of money to process water and make it safe. So far, the money has been used for other things. Soviet citizens are very worried about the effects of the water on themselves and their children.

Alcoholism and other kinds of drug abuse are common in the Soviet Union. In fact, no other nation on earth has such a high number of alcoholics. Soviet authorities point to alcoholism as the

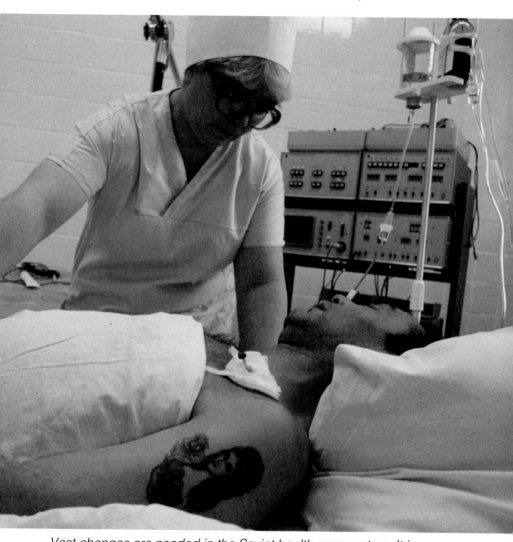

Vast changes are needed in the Soviet health-care system. It is so poor that some citizens have called it a source of national shame.

number one health problem in their country today. They say that frustration and the drabness of their lives make many Soviets turn to drinking as a way to forget their troubles.

Farmers, factory workers, soldiers—all kinds of people are affected. In some farming communities, work stops at two in the afternoon, and all the workers begin drinking. By evening, most of the community is drunk.

In factories, the same thing happens. Once the supervisor has made his or her rounds, the workers take bottles of vodka from their coats and lunch boxes. They drink steadily the rest of the day. Some even anchor themselves onto their workbenches. They use vice grips and secure their clothing so they do not become dizzy and call attention to themselves by falling.

When vodka or other kinds of liquor are not available, many Soviets drink substances that contain alcohol. In 1987 more than ten thousand people in the Soviet Union died from drinking perfume, jet fuel (often drunk by pilots), and shoe polish.

Health Care for a Bribe

For those citizens who are ill enough to need hospital treatment, there are additional problems. Many Soviet hospitals are surprisingly primitive for a nation that is considered a superpower in technology.

Most of the hospitals in the Soviet Union are free. In the communist system, health care is provided by the government, and no one is required to pay. Although the theory is attractive, in practice the system has many faults.

Because Soviet doctors and nurses are paid such low wages, they frequently try to get bribes from patients. A nurse may refuse to change bandages or give medicine, for instance, unless the patient pays. The bribe may range from a few dollars to several hundred.

Because the system depends more and more on illegal pay-offs, the care is unfair. Those who have no money to pay the bribes get little or no attention in hospitals. Soviet authorities call the situation "a catastrophe, a source of national shame."

Recently a law was passed that allows private hospitals to operate. Private hospitals charge for their services. Almost immediately Soviet citizens have noticed a big change. People find the private hospitals more modern and more efficient than those run by the state.

Most state hospitals in rural areas have no hot water. Almost one-third of the hospitals in the country have no indoor toilets. But all the private hospitals are equipped with these "luxuries."

Patients say they prefer paying for their health care and knowing beforehand what everything will cost. There are no bribes, no slipping money to doctors and nurses.

However, some doctors and nurses are fighting the law allowing private hospitals. They say that the new law goes against the idea of communism. Some Soviet citizens say that those medical workers are really more worried about keeping their payoffs coming in. In the months ahead, the Soviet Union will be deciding whether to continue to offer patients a choice of state and private hospitals.

Empty Drugstore Shelves

Still another health problem is the shortage of medicines in the Soviet Union. Many common remedies, such as cough syrup and aspirin, are in very short supply. In some communities they are unavailable.

The head of Moscow's health department estimated in 1990 that only about 400 out of 2,800 medications are available to Soviet pharmacies and doctors. Most of these medicines are made in Western nations. Many Soviets blame their government for not spending the necessary money to keep supplies on hand. Others blame the mountains of paperwork needed to order anything.

Many doctors have spoken out against the situation. Many complain that they must reuse disposable syringes. There simply are not enough of them to go around. Even though hospital workers try to scrub the needles with steel wool after each use, the syringes can still spread germs. The shortage has led to dozens of Soviet children being exposed to the virus that causes AIDS.

Many Soviets have pointed out that medicines are not luxuries. "We can survive without blue jeans or sausages or sugar," said one Soviet editor. "But we cannot live without medicine. People will not tolerate such shortages for long."

Stress from Within

The months and years ahead will be crucial ones for Gorbachev and the Soviet Union. On the horizon are new opportunities for peace with the United States. That is a big change from the

With the coming of glasnost, *many Soviet republics, like Lithuania, are demanding freedom and independence.*

past, when any capitalist nation was seen by the Soviet leaders as "the enemy."

But there are obstacles. Gorbachev must cope with Soviet citizens impatient for a better way of life. They are tired of being a military superpower with a backward economy.

Another obstacle is the explosive unrest in such Soviet republics as Georgia, Lithuania, and Azerbaijan. These republics are tired of being ruled by the Soviets. They believe that their people would be better off independent. Other republics are eager to change their boundaries. They maintain that the present political lines are artificial, that the lines cut right through ethnic communities.

Most of all, Gorbachev needs the strong support of his people. Although a lot of Soviets are eager for change, many fear it. They think a rapid change toward capitalism would cause suffering to those used to having the government take care of them. Gorbachev recently assured them that he is a good Communist and believes strongly in the ideas of Marx and Lenin. He also sees that the system needs to evolve, or change slowly, to meet the needs of his people.

"He's got the toughest job in the world," said one U.S. official. Perhaps Gorbachev would agree. At any rate, the world will be watching with interest the coming developments in the Soviet Union.

FACTS ABOUT THE SOVIET UNION

Capital: Moscow

Population: 287 million

Form of government: Communist dictatorship

Official language: Russian

Chief products:
  Agriculture: barley, beef cattle, corn, oats, potatoes
  Manufacturing: chemicals, electrical equipment, iron,
    steel, lumber

Glossary

black market *Buying and selling goods illegally, without the approval of the government.*

bureaucracy *A government that is slow moving because every action has to be approved by a lot of people and meet fixed rules.*

bureaucrat *An official who works by fixed rules, without using his or her own judgment.*

capitalism *An economic system based on private ownership of business and property.*

communism *An economic system based on the idea that all the people should share everything in their society. It does not allow private ownership of property.*

czar *An emperor.*

détente *A period of relaxed tensions between the United States and the Soviet Union during the 1970s.*

glasnost *"Openness." A program of honesty begun by Mikhail Gorbachev.*

kolkhoz *A collective farm in the Soviet Union. Many farms are combined to make one collective farm.*

peasant *A poor farmer.*

perestroika *"Restructuring." Gorbachev's goal for reorganizing the Soviet government and economy.*

purges *Mass arrests and killings during the time of Stalin.*

Renaissance *The rebirth of learning that took place in Western Europe beginning in the 14th century.*

republic *One of the 15 states that make up the Soviet Union.*

revolution *A sudden, often violent, change from one kind of government to another.*

serf *A poor farmer who was enslaved to a landowner during the time of the czars in Russia. Serfs were freed in 1861.*

sovkhoz *A very large state farm in the Soviet Union. The government owns and operates it, hiring workers to farm it.*

superpower *A country with a military force strong enough to dominate most other countries in the world.*

Index